FOXLOGIC, FIREWEED

Jennifer K. Sweeney

THE BACKWATERS PRESS

An imprint of the University of Nebraska Press

Acknowledgments for the use of copyrighted
material appear on pages ix–x, which
constitute an extension of the copyright page.

Library of Congress Cataloging-in-Publication Data
Names: Sweeney, Jennifer K. (Jennifer Kochanek) author.
Title: Foxlogic, fireweed / Jennifer K. Sweeney.
Description: Lincoln, Nebraska: The Backwaters Press,
an imprint of the University of Nebraska Press, [2020] |
Series: The Backwaters Prize in poetry
Identifiers: LCCN 2020004291
ISBN 9781496222695 (paperback)
ISBN 9781496223302 (epub)
ISBN 9781496223319 (mobi)
ISBN 9781496223326 (pdf)
Subjects: LCGFT: Poetry.
Classification: LCC PS3619.W4426 F69 2020 |
DDC 811/.6—dc23
LC record available at https://lccn.loc.gov/2020004291

Set in Fanwood by Laura Buis.
Designed by L. Auten.

CONTENTS

ACKNOWLEDGMENTS

Thank you to the editors who published poems from this collection, sometimes in different form.

Academy of American Poets: "Poem for My Son in the Car," "The Snow Leopard Mother"

The Adroit Journal: "The Game of Life"

Arroyo: "To Remain in Perhaps," "When we were carnies"

The Awl: "*bike shed* will often show more results than '*bike shed*'"

Burnside Review: "Letter from the Sound," "Snake in the Zendo"

Cimarron Review: "Ceremony"

Construction: "The Day Everywhere and White," "Duet" as "Poem"

Crab Creek Review: "Foxlogic, Fireweed," "The Pear Trees at Terezín"

Cutthroat: "Cabinet of Curiosities"

DMQ *Review*: "Tree; Tremble," "Eclipse" as "When we moved to the desert"

Kenyon Review Online: "Crickets, Vespers"

The Los Angeles Review: "Antlers," "Bat Milk"

Linebreak: "The Somnambulist"

Love's Executive Order: "Making Use"

Mississippi Review: "For the brown widow who laid her eggs under my son's bicycle seat," "Outside My Window Is a Window," "What Turkeys Can Teach Us about Grief in Suburbia"

The Offending Adam: "Old Town Square"

Paris-American: "How Many Leaves and Boats Gather Together"

Passages North: "Meeting," "Still Life with Skeleton and Sight Word"

Ping-Pong: "Preface"

Pleiades: "Variation on Bear and Moon"

Queen of Cups: "Altar: Aerial Heart," "Altar: Compass," "Altar: Fairytale"

Rust + Moth: "Jennifers of the 1970s," "Picking Up My Wedding Dress"

South Dakota Review: "I am driving a whale heart"

Spillway: "A Deer Story," "Cul-de-sac," "Our Laundry Room of Deflated Balloons"

Stirring: "Landslide"

Terrain: "In the House of Seals," "Nacelle and Turn," "Vigil," "Wildest"

Thrush: *"I will break into my life for my life"*

ANTHOLOGIES:

"Tinderbox" appears in *Orangelandia: The Literature of Inland Citrus*, edited by Gayle Brandeis (Inlandia Institute, 2014).

"Still Life with Djembe and Black Widow" appears in *Still Life with Poem: Contemporary Natures Mortes in Verse*, edited by Jehanne Dubrow and Lindsay Lusby (The Literary House Press, 2016).

"Duet" and "Still Life with Skeleton and Sight Word" appear in Lit-FUSE: 10 Years, edited by Michael Schein (Cave Moon Press, 2016).

"In the House of Seals" and "Snake in the Zendo" appear in *Know Me Here: An Anthology of Poetry by Women*, edited by Katherine Hastings (WordTemple Press, 2017).

"The Day Everywhere and White" and "In the House of Seals" appear in *Fire and Rain: Ecopoetry of California*, edited by Lucille Lang Day and Ruth Nolan (Scarlet Tanager Press, 2018).

"Pastoral" was originally my answer to an interview question from Donna Vorreyer published on her blog, *Put Words Together. Make Meaning*, August 10, 2015.

"To Remain in Perhaps" was printed as a broadside for *Broadsided* in April 2018, edited by Elizabeth Bradfield.

FOXLOGIC,
FIREWEED

1

(WHOLE FLOCKS OF RAIN)

Letter from the Sound

Faraway, famous bird
who knows where the time goes?
Gone fishing, gone down
the waterloo good-time party boat
in my own little sadsong head.
The rain here is staggering and instrumental.
Whole flocks of rain
fall briefly at sunset
which never comes or comes
only in its absence, the bell ringing
and the vespers empty of monks.
When I am away so long
I become habitual, each morning
return to the first ventured waters.
I enlist my characters
assign my guideposts.
Peony. Cricket. Chime.
Wet yawn in the wind, a bow to the rock scree
as if I have lived here forever
the nothing-queen, the crater dream
crossing mercy in my blue coat of rain.
Perhaps you have been here too?
Softly lit by candles emptying yourself
with such dedication
the journal pages creased to paper
boats, still waiting
for transformation.

I will break into my life for my life

Headline:
"Woman Accidentally Joins Search Party Looking for Herself."

A woman on a bus.
A woman buying milk.
You can go missing,
whispering Surtsey, your finger running
across the map's lava fields.
To fade into the measure of daily noise:
sometimes a relief, unbecoming
sometimes a spill, bleeding out.
A volcano in winter.
Strange birds everywhere.
Surtsey makes your hands tender
things in pockets. Praise
watching a man in a foreign post office
threefold a letter and shimmy it
into the envelope.
Praise the clarity of running
a brush through hair at a road stop.
Running the hot and cold
which are both cold, you can go
pulling at a shirt's loose threads.
And over Styrofoam coffee,
a woman is gone, everyone agrees.
Hearing her story from a distance
you do not recognize the woman is you
and they do not recognize the woman is you.
Who would not join the search?
No one is sure of her

name, but you hold its possibility
in your mouth. You want to chase her
out of the night. She has come
a long way and you don't
want her to miss the flood
basalt, the delicacy of ash
you tongue in the air.

Bat Milk

They do, they do—
inside the living mountain

where night is a constant—
curl up like a god's

shuttered eye
and wait as I waited

body of my body
we sing the same

blood-warm song.
Casements wrapped in ink

they are to themselves
the center of the earth

by which all things
distinguish

though still they may ask
as I have asked

staring across
the battered plain

what monster what
monster am I?

Midwife of shadow
the first milk breath

hums in the mineral sky.

Poem for My Son in the Car

The wipers sweep two overlapping hills
on the glass, we are quiet against

    the squeaky metronome as we often are
    before the concerns of the day well up.

Today: *Is it dark inside my body?*
The wet cedar's dark of green-gone-black

    of damp earth mending itself,
    a pewter bell rung into night's collected

sigh, choral and sleep-sunk.
Dark as the oyster's clasp

    in its small mottled pocket
    and the word *pocket* a tucked notion

set aside in-case-of.
Inside there are vestibules, clapboards

    trapdoors, baskets,
    there is cargo,

there is the self carrying the self
sprint, trodden—

    no where does it not—
    and mournful as a spine bowing to wood

you carry your actions; inside
is cave and concern,

    everything purposeful
    heartwood, clockwork, crank and tender

iron in the mountain belly,
all the hidden things breathing.

    Outside of and woven into, you are
    the knowledge you can't touch

the desire you can't locate,
unnameable questions unnameable answers,

    source and tributary
    and the rivers that hold you

beneath. Your darkness
lives in that potential,

    snowblind
    aurora

pulse
shore.

Outside My Window Is a Window

For years I needed to be in motion
the first to get up and leave
the one who kept on walking

like I needed to walk until I understood
I existed. More tangible than talk
I crossed my city from one end to the other

bay to shore and back, crossed
Prague and Indiana and the abandoned
railway line to the bird sanctuary

to the warehouse scattered with sequins
and feathers where they made drag movies
at night, window into window, crossed

a mountain in Oregon until I nearly stepped
on a rattlesnake then I turned
around and walked back again,

as if walking were a kind of breathing.
Metronome, sway, the path
a heartstep, it hurt to stop

then not. What changed
but a key slipping into a knot
and staying became the bearable thing.

Art of the window, glass scrim,
to be both the measured eye
of the canvas and the one

appraising the scene.
Crows on a pomegranate tree.
A neighbor giving his boy

a shave on the porch.
When I lived in Michigan
it rained every Monday for three months

and I ran to the window
hearing the garbage truck's rhythmic screech,
like a child, though I was 35,

watching the wet truck heave its claw arms
toward everything I had cast away,
week after week,

throwing away the weight
of myself in ten-gallon bags,
the same tired men pulling up

and hauling it away.
I'm knocking against the pane,
I want to see toward you and beyond

you, the door in the meadow,
aperture in the fog.
A dog pulls a man on skis

along the blizzard sidewalk,
a skunk stripes the brief frame
and absorbs back into the night.

Outside my window is a window
radial sundial scrim—
in seeing I cast toward

the person I was, toward
mountain, mercenary, the tremble
of wind through grasses;

in perceiving, they cast back
a yes quiet enough to startle the atoms.
That we might move between distances,

past and present,
inside the self and out.
It is not a small thing

to be the quiet eye,
the furthering step
or that this exchange is worth something,

never knowing why a grief came
or left and never knowing
all those who have steadied us there

watching or passing
unlocking each other silently
with our little keys of witness.

Crickets, Vespers

beyond the terribly bright and curious tender
we know what little and much the grass knows
gods in charge of holy nothing but to keep
reaching toward all-space
salt meadow   skin of the ghost wave
rising
keep the bandwidth of our chatter slow
everslow the rain falling into its own perception
there are more ways to listen than weep
slow the cricket nocturne, a human lifespan
hear our voices sing back
angels in the field
clock clock
what have we come for

Old Town Square

Prague

Death shakes his hourglass at noon.
The cobblestone maze sways with accents.

I lose direction.
Lightning threads the sky,

a sea of marionettes float in slow motion.
Hollow limbs rooted to strings

and those heavy sleeping heads
condemned to a smile or frown.

Voices wash over,
words I will never understand.

An anonymous love swells and empties
for everything I do not know.

A string tugs memory, wrist.
My story keeps me treading the same air.

The Pear Trees at Terezín

1.

To talk about the pear trees at Terezín I must
first talk about wandering off course, a heavy
wood and the sky darkening, how coming upon
a monastery's orchard steeply embedded
in the hillside, *fog nesting, tangled grain,*
I could sense it sensing the mist, the bell tower,
reaching with the palpable leaf-reach
of breathing, and by the time the rain drove
there were two of us under a shack's roof,
thick stripes of water raking down
the corrugated tin.

Peering through that wet lens, pale bulbs *bodies*
dripping greenly, I thought *softest parts blushing*
but said nothing to the woman beside me,
our voices lushly silent, having stumbled
into this accidental pact in tenderness,
and when it was finished enough to step
forward into that wet light,
she bounding up and I down, I felt her hand
on my shoulder though it was not there
folded into the clarity and blur, quiet sky now
but each tree gathering pear-rain.
To be perceived by an orchard, taken
into its green eye is to receive
the answer to a question I did not know
enough to ask.

2.

To talk about my grandmother's pear tree
I must first talk about boxes,
how my eldest sister passed her clothes down to my middle
and she to me and when they were thrice-worn
we brought them to our grandmother who sent them
to relatives in Poland who lived in a house with a dirt floor.
Running my finger across the small country on the globe,
I felt a blanket of spores, cool mud molded to the arches
of their feet, not unlike our feet, these other girls
outfitted in our pilled wool and souvenir T-shirts.

At Christmas she brought home Eucharist
and after eggnog gave us each a piece.
Were you not a priestess to us in your living room
tearing bites of god-wafer for the new year?

And who planted the first doubt-seed?
Who set it in motion warped and grafted
through a lineage of hard life? No one
shares this shadow but leaves attic clues,
small cries of evidence from a scrapbook
or boxed letter as when we found photos
with her face scratched off,
one where she'd trimmed herself out
with sewing scissors, or a boy in each hand,
face poked out with a pencil
then neatly sleeved in the album.

Clouds barrel over Prague castle and I steal for the orchard.
It is my rain-place, happy to create any kind of history

feels like the body drawing back to a shape.
Nuns lop branches in thunder light, silver arms
scissoring deadwood while one hides behind a trunk,
wipes juice from her chin, gathering pears in the belly
of her habit and it could be my grandmother pinning
blouses to a clothesline, picking pears from the tree that died
when she died, pears that tasted like wet sand and sunlight,
or my grandmother gathering sweaters from the branches,
pinning a row of pears to the line.

Why do I feel this only now,
arms heavy in my wet blouse, feet in the mud.
We live so far away from our stories and barely touch them.

3.

To talk about my grandmother I must first talk
about the girl who slept through the lightning storm.
Shaded bench, a thick tree
in need of pruning and her body untouched
by rain. She must have been a runaway,
docile, snoring, curled against the Communist concrete.
I couldn't imagine her exhaustion
having long ago shucked the allowances
of public and private nor her comfort
for she did not once clench her duffel or
brace against the battering wind;
in a susurrant baritone, she hummed
leagues beneath any surface.
I want to say it was her confidence
(need, terror) to so completely let go
of herself that made me watch, the storm
a dream against the wheel that brought her here,
and it was also my grandmother who, at twelve,
changed her difficult Polish name
applying for a library card when she could not
bear to say her name, she said *Viola*,
womanish instrument and so it was,
written in block script by the librarian, the word
cast into her future on its sturdy musical hook.

How many times did she save herself like that?
In what sun-ripened field did she harvest her warmth?
In a country where someone is asking my name,
I think   *Boxed   Sleeved   Covered-in-earth*
one life barreling forward while the other
withers in a scrapbook.

To be so given over to the body as to forget it entirely
on a train, in a question, benchside as thunder churns.
When the sun cracks through, it lights a pear
heavy over her head and she wakes up dry.
I smile. Point up. Say *Viola*.

4.

To talk about wandering off course I must talk
about how it began raining when the tour bus brought us
to the internment camp in Terezín.
Raining when they packed us into confinement
to share the wet ash of breath,
in the black light of the Red Cross propaganda film,
and as we marched
single file through an underground maze
toward an execution wall.
I mean both that it rained and it rained
inside my body. I had nothing
to offer in return but a wet thump
of sorrow. The artists were stolen
here, the painters, poets, the musicians
scribbling librettos in the dark.
Darkest hour. A children's opera. An art class
hidden in a suitcase. They were forced
to build the railroad that dragged them
to Krakow. We stood inside rooms of death
and singing and all we could do was stand.
My hands were never so empty as they were
in Terezín. And there were baby swallows
nesting in the cell eaves.
We were touched by this, desperate
for any easy token: *Neutral to history, life goes on,*
but the swallows had nothing to do with Terezín.
After we left the execution wall, we passed a pear tree
full of ripe fruit, growing, rotting, weeping back.
Gray-green the ground wet and fallen,
gray-green the leaves.
Some women with giant cameras
wandered off course, stood under that tree

and brought the flesh to their mouths, they ate
the earth of that place, the sap of it grafted within.
Smiled. One said *I was surprised it tasted sweet!*
Yes, the others agreed. *It had been delicious.*
It distracted me a while to judge them.
To leave with some stupid thing decided.
No one has ever eaten a pear from that tree.
It will always be raining in Terezín.

Altar: Compass

how one morning the air
felt different
what was blurred had become
a thing you wanted to arrange
an orange scarf
a pine cone
thick curl of bark
when placed downward
made a textured hill
a spoonful of seeds
six pebbles in a line
you could not remember
since when a small act had brought
such pleasure

Alpenhorn

Assemble the tree of it, peakside,
blond light against
mutual whites of this winter altitude.
If the mountain could play itself,
if blue fog breathed inside alpine
the singular awl of loneliness
calling *buried-stars-empty-pockets*
out of its wood-rich alpenwomb.
In the gloaming of the bone
blow the winding shallows home.
I had never heard it
but when I heard it—
one slope breath seeking—
it was the fleet-sound I came from,
whatever pulse spun in me located
and I knew where to find my shadow
among the shadows.

Wildest

The hour of snacks and homework
and we're enlarging the world with adverbs of scale.
See how easily smooth becomes smoother,
how we can silk it farther to the sheen that is most
itself. You are taller, stronger, a little farther
from my center, but not farthest
(may we stop here in the horizon note of *farther*)
and you want to know how accretion applies to wild.
One field left longer, one never entered
by anything that sought to change it.
Say *wild* and the honeysuckle curls round the cedar
and the cedar's silence mats a soft floor in winter
whose most faithful withholding buckles
the cloudhead. Say *wilder* and it's less
bewildering, more why,
the cloud funneling now, the animals hurried
into the barn, and we're left
staring at the floodwaters salting our questions.
Wilder rakes its impulsive hand over us
and we ride off the road in the night.
And *wildest*, what sprung cosmos is that?
I hope we never see it enough to know
as here in this measured plot we keep turning
the hose on the fire ants and they dutifully
froth up. Somewhere lives expanses
never perceived, deepest praise
all the lost coasts, outbacks, untrodden
tundras of this world, its earths too wild
to survive us. My boy wants to know
how wild it gets. As long as there is land

that has never breathed in
our borrowed must of oxygen,
then the mandrakes quiver in their sacs;
as you curl into sleep, the dryad
is out there pressing her most unburdened head
against evening's northest altar.

2

(I AM DRIVING A WHALE HEART)

Preface

You could say *heavy as an elephant*
but not to the elephant
whose thunder is a lean O
as her speed makes a wind
across the diehard plain
and the flags of her ears
undulate and slap
like rockweed
against the tide
but not to the rockweed
whose undulations depend
on the long note of sleep
that makes the sea,
those flickering silhouettes
knee-deep in moon-shavings
who know nothing of elephants.

I am driving a whale heart

In the dome of its body the blue
whale has a heart large
as a Honda Civic, its soft engine
pumping throngs of blood

in the equator deep.
Whaleblood. Whaleheart.
These words open a little salt-rusted
door in me. I want sometimes

to sit by the wooden boy's fire
in the cave-belly and fold into a song
and its forgetting. Like crawling
into baritone sleep after the body

exhausted from use. After
the body I never knew
was a mothering kind of creature.
I have wanted to be inside the whale's

dream, the way the sugar ant wants
to crawl inside my own heart and feast.
I left home in a whale heart
drove it through blizzards,

off the side of the road, straight
across the country trading coasts
for no good reason than to change
my life as much as I could.

Largest heart, Deepest diver,
your blood its own ten-ton sea,

traveling hundreds of miles a day
in the ship of your body

sounding your single horn
to preserve your solitude.
Chugging toward black rock, black hills
and the carved-out drop of badlands,

my offkey songs another dry slap
against the windshield.
Hydranths in the cloudhead,
which current to follow in the rising dark?

Windmills became mineral plains,
whales floating above the salt flats.
I ran to them but they disappeared
in my arms. Driving my fish-heart

into the yellow headlands' tinderbox
of dead grasses, the baited questions
were already hooking my future.
In the corner of a borrowed room,

I dealt a haphazard astrology:
If Perseids dripped from the eucalyptus
If a film about tide pools was projected onto the fog
If the basin proved to be fertile

then I'd stay in San Francisco. No memory
anywhere in my wake.
I think now it was not where I landed
but the story of the leaving.

Before I knew how to be inside my life,
rootstock in the daily,
what I loved most was careening
toward the idea of it,

never the stark arrival,
fumbling with knifed keys
in the shadows, stepping
over the gray pool

of mail with its terrible small weight,
but one foot in the swirl,
those brief seconds of lift
before the tide pulled me in.

When you washed ashore, *Largest*,
it took four men to pull the heart
from your body, they wanted to see it
hauled from the depths.

It would take 640 male hearts to make yours.
It would take the starry plough
culled from the mountain
to know anything about you at all.

And then it's ten years, twenty,
and my body it's been the good sea,
though suddenly, never alone again
so that when waiting

in a doctor's annual office
I can be seized by the floodwaters—
the canned triumph of a pop song,
a plastic seashell in a decaying aquarium—

the wire so easily tripped.
When everyone is briefly accounted for

I plunge into epiphany,
slipping out to fetch the godly bills,

the dollar grocery papers, waxy catalogs
that locate me across every migration
and something in the way the domed sky
shivers with its palpable fade

or I am exhausted
to the point of sheer openness,
it returns me to the gasp
of emerging from that car's

salt-rusted door at Land's End
shedding grain by grain
in the surf. Cold bare feet
on the cul-de-sac asphalt

I crawl into my whale heart,
pocked and peeling now,
that place where love
was sourced in loneliness,

for a single breath, medicinal sip
of beyond, licking salt
from my fingers
in my own private hum

before returning
to the buoyant voices
the small hands reaching up
toward their idea of mother.

Wind under the Skin

house full of crickets   moon
slung low in the birches

good night the clock
with its one good eye

do not keep watch
over the tossing bed

the uncorked wine   a wind
large as a country

roils up the coast
we will wake to hacked

cedars and silence
the locked door

buckles   crickets
scatter the floor

like dropped coins
how much

of the body is sail
how much anchor?

Picking Up My Wedding Dress

I circled the city block farther out,
parked beneath the highway overpass
next to a huddle of cardboard
shelters and walked the six blocks alone.
What I liked most about San Francisco:
it was such a good place to be alone in.
I tried on the dress one last time and again
the seamstress tried to stuff my chest
with the padded cups. Like afternoon scones,
I refused them before, polite at first,
but always her hand reaching for my neckline,
smile with no smile in it, something
forceful between us. I tossed them
by the circular mirror
multiplying into puddles of milk.
To walk back into the gray sketch of that day
with so much satin and my casual panicked
face, as if carrying a tent or ream enough
to clothe a family, who was I to hold it,
I could not hold it, folding and unfolding
in my arms and trying also not to drag it
on the lived-in sidewalk, crossing
streets in a final moment of most singular
aloneness before not, past graffiti fences,
shag-boarded clubs. Next to the car, a man
squatting with his pants off, yelling
at everything, and I stood across
from him in the salt and fecal air
with that white white sea-of-my-body
that had been for weeks

so carefully fitted to each slight curve,
I was someone who had been *attended to*,
the dress holding me then as the bay wind
was also holding me pinned to concrete
where I could not look away.

Variation on Bear and Moon

I will now play this fog as a cello
I will play this dogwood
as a crisis this too granite I will play
my hands as prologue
this matterhorn as a matterhorn
I will be the conductor and you
will be the moon   see how
our bodies under the sea
of covers make a blue present
play morning as a theory
of erosion   a harbinger of heat
stand up in my hollowed body
your wooden shoes
aren't all boulders wonderfully
erratic? here comes one now clumsy
with matter I will play it
as a bear lumbering in the alpine
you floodsong rockfall
mirror in my wine glass I will play
the nothing of it gold when the tide is going
send the throat stone down
send the cold moan downriver

Jennifers of the 1970s

We were part of a tribe, at least three
to a class, you could scan a room and find us
everywhere, swishing a Hula Hoop around
our Jennifer hips. Enough of us to populate
Fiji or Damascus, we orbited our own planet,
the paisley atmosphere swirling as the bell
bottoms tolled and the skyrockets took flight.
Mirrored disco ball, each facet released another
known in relation to the initials of our last names
latch-hooked on yarn pillows, ironed on
to the back of our concert gut-shirts.
Macrame belt, god's eye,
we came out of a Dreamsicle,
reigned like corn husk girls easily wrapped
into skirts at the church bazaar.
Our decade was barefoot, tapestry, buttercup,
lemon-lime, rickrack, Easy Cheese.
To be so abundant, bearing a name that everyone
agreed was lovely, a triple note they wanted
to repeat, I stopped hearing it, the swift hook
of the J, little gem in the mouth, the soft fur
landing, all folded in the envelope of the common.
A Xanadu of Jennifers,
A roller rink of Jennifers,
A decahedron of Jennifers,
I could always see the collective of us.
Unwittingly part of the ensemble yet to be one
meant we were also gifted an alter ego, a spray-on leotard
or chameleon foil lurking under our jumpers.
I run into one of us now in yoga pants,

maybe a child at the hip. We're tired, we've seen
some things but we're pointed to the horizon,
and sometimes a few of us still rise
when the latte order is called and our gently wrinkling
faces smile knowingly. Glitter wave
we all came out of so decisively,
we're the Fosse dance in the musical that gets
revived in summer community theater,
the cake still holding its layers in the rain,
the silver moon boot that flares
in the late October sky.

In the House of Seals

Año Nuevo Lighthouse ruins

Abandoned on its eroded jetty,
the Victorian is gutted by windbreak,
waves and the pale ash
of salt and plaster.
A clean wind howls up the spiral
stair, rattling the vacant dumbwaiter,
the picture window, walls
bleached in sheets of raw sun.
What keeper's lantern once swung
the veranda to meet the shore-
tossed plot, what wrack
and beckon of Pacific tide
is now pilgrimage for elephant seals.
Given a home, they return
to the mecca of their kind
paddle into the blown-out façade
to birth and die
in heaps of tender slack, skin
like buckled wallpaper.
Dear sitting rooms of milk and bone:
life keens starkly forward
while the dying nurse the dead.
Who knows what bright ruins
might lean from the pitch
of night to shelter us?
To be so wanted
in the work of decay.

If given a home, I'll take this home.
If given a soul, I'll shepherd it
on the backs of seals
held in the bellows
of a graysound love.

To Remain in Perhaps

Whatever the great *it* of your life
it may not happen, you know that,

withholding every third seed of breath,
and despite the outcome, afterward

you will feel better and worse.
The tar pits of La Brea are flecked

with iridescence. You might say
how beautiful and shiny the tar

but if your attention is keen
you'd see the dragonflies

sticking themselves to the hot
flats like carefully formed mistakes.

Welcome to flux.
The roofs are made of rice paper

and there are train tracks laid over the sand
going straight into the ocean.

Every morning we boarded our little ship

though our travels could not brag of anything
but the minor. Most days we never made it
out of the bottle.

Mimosa seedpods like a switch
of leather between our thumbs,
snails sheening across the sidewalk

in a brief and silver art,
we were pirates of seeing
the quiet thing. We rooted for the ants

who found the colored sugar spill
hauling emeralds across the kitchen counter.
We praised the black widow who fastened

five starry sacs against the clanger of the bell.
My life, my agenda, how it hurt to pry
off that pronoun like a swollen cork

but when its absence became a comfortable
wound, (my) life kept its borders
open, relieved of the burden

of definition.
We aimed our twiggy arrows at the sun,
fed animals with our hands,

and with a clan privacy ate dinner on the floor.
It was hard not to slip into nostalgia
while still immersed:

confusing the tenses when I cast behind
what was present as if to prepare
myself for the years ahead

when they would orbit outward
from the focus of our choral gaze.
I am supposed to say I wanted

to devour them, I wanted to run away,
that I was tired and worn
like a groove, and sometimes

I wanted to read all day and mostly
I wore sweatpants
and sometimes I yelled and everything

was dreadfully unclean, but being with my sons
every day was most like theater snow,
a tiny hidden source above our heads

cranking out the dust, always a shock
how it lit up the dark.
Terrible cliché, I knew it would go fast,

could feel the gallop beneath our perpetual
chase game. True, my life, good horse,
trotted back as I was warned it would

not, rearranged in fractals
and without the same iron grasp.
And when I said how much

I loved the hours: the concerning stares,
I was a helicopter, I was a bore,
surely obsessed, I must have lost

my feminist edge somewhere in the Lego bin
but before the world got a piece of them
we were in a snow globe, a glass womb

filled with the amniotic of our own awe.
We were mighty and no one saw us.
We rescued lizards from a sudden cold,

we made drums out of every single thing.
We hid from each other and told each other
where we were hiding.

The Somnambulist

Flight of the marsh queen, winter
branching from her head
topsy over the starhatch.
Glaze and grit, the oatgrass
carries the hunter's
moon cross the meadow,
the oatgrass bluesy and eternal.
Come round, come whether-or-not.
The fog rises from the ground,
so much moth-light and brine,
comforting and strange
like waking in an underwater photo.
Is it foxlogic? Fireweed?
On what foreign terms
do I keep arriving
hours past midnight
in this lucid province?
Blackwing, little wind,
how will it be to say
brightly into the thrum
I beat I beat
my water drum?

3

(BRIGHTEN THE ROAD, DEAR)

Duet

Begin with five words.
Chickaree. Sockwitch. Matterhorn. Burro. Styx.
I stretch them across the flatline and wait for a spark
and if this act of listening is useless
as standing in a field inventing doors
then come, my little failures, meet me
in a gift shop in the middle of nowhere
where cheap clock hands spin circles of air.
Let me cradle you in the cold
disk of a hot pink seashell, slip
inside your rickety wooden shoes
and charm no-thing and its counter-thing.
I have no strings. I have no fire.
But I can sit roadside for hours
watching the hawks chase the crows—
who says habit isn't original?
The wet eye, the being
its small measure of daily noise.
Hum and the grass trembles.

When we were carnies

We kept odd hours in the desert,
midnight when the heat lifted like a zeppelin
we bundled in layers and lit the lamppost.

You oiled the hinges, anchored rebar
with the heel of your work boot
while I swept sand from the loveseats

with a feather brush.
We couldn't keep playa dust
out of the phonograph

though we fashioned a small tent from a kite.
Tom Waits, a grainy *Que Sera*
sent our message to the ether

as we manually pushed the empty
carousel, slow panels of night
swinging in tilted circles.

Keepers of the rust, the turning,
of peeled-paint goddesses
with their drastic faces.

We took our guests' hands gingerly,
tucked them into Shiva's bosom
with army blankets and flasks of whiskey,

gold teeth gleaming
as we wheeled the ride forward.
When it got up speed,

you kissed me long and dizzy,
and the carousel unwound from its axis,
spun out into the dark.

Still Life with Djembe and Black Widow

After the djembe fell on the baby
I exiled it behind the easy chair
as I did so many objects made newly hazardous,

every beyond and out-of-reach crevice
a still life for scissors, candlesticks, binder clips.
I never learned to put anything

properly away. After the djembe
stopped presenting its call and response,
some weeks passed, it could have been one

or fifty, I slept and did not sleep,
the baby learned to walk, the brother to read,
soon the chairs were exiled to the garage, anything

that could be climbed, the baby
wanted to hook the moon in the chandelier,
could ladder a bookcase in under a minute.

A living room is a diorama and a black forest.
Stashed, dormant, all the unsung cornered things
I did not see balanced like rock sculptures,

one hand lifted I did not remember to beat
against any hollow, a low-grade
amnesia of hiding and forgetting, I was a thief

and I was the thieved.
Much of mothering is to focus in
so myopically on *keeping safe,*

lens that keeps clicking the eye closer
until objects become furred and constellated
in their own radical space systems. Solar-me,

there were no chairs anymore, we were spinning
in the all-day tumble of being
in a body. And when I finally dragged

it back out, the djembe's
skin was a dust-layer I clapped
sounding us all into focus, a single bass

that drew us toward,
and when we began again to feel
the furred edge of its skin, the sleek

unruly goblet of it, a network
of cobwebs clarified under the binding;
gazing in, gauzy circles stretched

across the void, a single bass
that drew forth a cluster of black widows
dizzy across the floor

I pressed and brought to the door,
finding here then another, I had to see
into their sleeping I had to keep waking.

Spider in the drum Spider in the drum
we chanted, which sounded like remembering
which sounded like falling.

The Day Everywhere and White

Spring and the world
is only a little bit dead,
but here we are

throwing away the dust.
Cast the eye cleanly
against the horizon, a snow

of cottonwood
hazing the plumb line.
March is a fly-by-night bird,

her eggs hidden
in tiny wells.
My thunder My thunder

Swing low when the moon is void.
Soon the heat will go platinum,
novice lizards dropping from the sky.

What good then, this huddle
of poppies drowsing the nothing
hillside. What good,

with moss on our hands.
Here where we need to water
down the water,

let's make a tree from a tree.
This yellow leaf
is just a little clue.

Snake in the Zendo

Folded as letters about failure
from the future, we are too serious
in our attempt, wall-facing,
arranging small pillows with mudra hands.
Grace is not practicing being graceful;
it's emerging from the scrim of every discomfort
with greater discomfort.
Once I wept in my car and a woman knocked on my window,
then held me in the gray parking lot morning.
It was not extraordinary but when I grip the steering wheel
in terror, I see her hands reaching toward the glass.
Make everything part of the practice, the zenji says,
jay that swipes your toast,
cleaning toilets in the guest house,
forest fire sweeping down the valley
the monks rush to meet, unraveling their black robes
of fire hose. Until the sobbing starts.
A woman in the corner whose body
shudders whole each grief shock and wave.
Collective we, great erasure,
do we imagine we are shouldering her grief
in a silent and beautiful gesture or are we trying
so hard to do something right we have surrendered
compassion in the stone of the Buddha?
The zenji's reed snaps its mindful warning
against the wood floor as she sobs
the meditation predawn into day,
our eyes coolly down.

And the morning after she left, a snake
slid its copper into the zendo,
between us, wall-facing, so dutiful.
Some kept sitting though most shrieked, ran out.
Oh we passed our judgment around
the breakfast table after with talk
of koans. I let the jay take the toast
from my mouth like spitting out sacrament.
The snake could have been a metaphor
but it was also a snake.
Blood in the lotus, we were trying so hard
in our unhappiness and the mountains
were beautiful crumbling under an opera
of fire. If there was anything to hear,
keep afraid what is fearful,
hold what demands to be held.

Tree; Tremble

Before: *terroir*
the wine-rich drink of earth
I have wanted to bend down
and taste holy in the mineral
and also, *terror* as a kind of joy
towering beyond study.
I send up my questions on a pulley
and they float away.
Between every sentence and its story
is a door
Between movement and air
a departure
Between prayer and sleep
is a loneliness so tidy
it doubles as contentment
Between every form and its arc
ripples a call from its dark center.
Shallow shutter swept
(what music folds between)
lapping at the shore of your feet
shaped by the sound
of the thing knocking against itself
in the living air.

Cul-de-sac

Sometimes you do not know you are having
a conversation. It is between you and another
but you haven't come toward

and entered the skin of it yet. When the wild
umbrage of the peach tree gilded and fell,
three silver birds were exposed in the branches.

Doves, I thought from a distance, the ones
whose mourning call I've been sounding back
all summer. Coming closer, they remained

nestled at home in the thicket, and closer,
suddenly too silver, my idea of them
went up in flight as I reached toward the metallic

light. Three cans crushed into bodies
I loosened from the tangle, 40 oz. Modelos,
wondering what late wanderer had settled

in the cul-de-sac to perch his drink.
It was winter then spring, the tree
flushed with hundreds of pink blossoms

and more mornings than not I pulled the can down—
what did it mean?—and again it returned.
Not knowing the other part of the ritual,

to see it became a kind of hello,
the exchange, less threat, more animal pact
the way a fox leaves dead squirrels

in its reliable patch of matted grass
and I roll them with sticks to the woods
having learned to manage the stiff weight.

Strange, understood without confrontation,
any conversation can be whittled down to
I am here, You are here,

the familiar becoming endearment until one day
it ceased after more than a year.
The fox retreated or was eaten, I was left

with my windy *I am here*
dragging across the air, staring
into the branches so thick they basket

the sky scanning for a metallic wing
glinting in the shade, a mourning call
I could reach up and echo back,

the question having shivered away,
question that kept asking if only
for the pleasure of being answered.

The Game of Life

Created in 1860 as "The Checkered Game of Life"

First, that we all lived in convertibles,
tucked our certain pink or blue genders
in like pushpins and sprung our lives in the highway's
metaphor, and what could go wrong
too was tidy, portioned out in the acceptable idea
of what could go wrong, a lost job or car accident
that would be statistically rebounded
by climbing Mount Everest or the family horse winning derby.
We collected mates, again certain our pink or blue
choices; to get married was to open the passenger door,
though sometimes I moved the peg of me
over so my blue man could drive.
And children were spawned shortly after
without pregnancy or labor, just dropped
into one of the available holes from the sky.
If you had more kids than holes, the directions suggested
crowding them in as you would in real life.
Real life we knew little about but took Milton Bradley's
word for it traversing small mountain ranges
meant to symbolize law school, taking out insurance policies,
collecting promissory notes; *promissory* a new word
I thought sounded religious.
And that we were trying to win at this, move through it faster
than the other eight-year-olds, arrive first
at our retirement nursing homes so we could secure
a room with a window at Millionaire Acres and finally begin
what then, real life?

Gathered on shag carpet with processed cheese,
we did not know that blue could abuse pink,
that pink would earn less than blue on Pay Day,
that pink could fall in love with pink, or blue with blue,
and that if you were pink or blue and also black
you would live under the suspicious gaze
of those who were not.
Rooting for our dice to fall
only on the good, indoctrinated again
and again into goodness, we did not know
what an art messing up a life could be, how you could
dent it, drain it dry in a full-flung collapse
and somehow rasp a weary breath in and watch
it eventually take hold. No mental illness,
no notion of the spectrum or drug rehab,
there were no swinger parties where everyone swapped cars
in the *Game of Life* yet there were spaces neatly reserved
every eighth of the journey where you could take revenge
on any of your mates for no good reason priming us
for opportunism, for ruthless neighborly cheer.
Rooting for the high spin, racing to the End
where "happy old age" beckoned in the corner opposite infancy,
to park at the *Day of Reckoning* where the last tapered years
forked into *millionaire* or *bankruptcy*, nothing in between
what could be measured in polarity, the game of mockery
in a final yes or no, and we wanted that greedy yes,
that glittery good finish, to have slipped through the whole ruck
unscathed, unravaged by any veer or rupture in the safe story,
we were at the clean beginnings of our devastation,
heading out toward the mild hills hoping for nothing
special but to park at the unlit horizon.

Landslide

Some mornings are delivered as if by bulldozer,
excavator, the piston's boom arm cranking
night away, dawn dumped from the backhoe's
toothed bucket. Five a.m. and a dead mouse
at our feet, the toilet's overflowed,
and the boy's weeping at the terrible
lack of dragons. This morning is a dragon
spitting us back into the daily.
Come on coffee grounds, be extraordinary.
Or every morning is like this. Or
this is how I love it most. Coming apart
and all at once. The unraveling
what is recalled best of childhood:
snakes in the basement, paint in my hair,
tying a string of bikes together and riding
downhill. I don't remember the crash,
just the calamitous liftoff. That knowledge
revealed only in the moment after pushing forward,
and the thrill of how much it would fail.

Eclipse

When we moved to the desert
we had to learn its vocabulary:
paloverde, cholla,
ocotillo like vertebrae
trying to lie down in the dirt.
We had to dodge tumbleweeds
under the overpass
measure the days in gradients of fire.
It's a dry heat
said the bleached bones walking the playa.
Rattlesnake, coachwhip, red racer.
Slid skins curled in the garage.
We removed cactus needles with duct tape,
alligator lizards from our kitchen,
we had to blackout the rooms.
In sheets, then blankets, wood blinds,
our efforts ever weighted,
we orchestrated an eclipse
to harness the available dark,
stashed it in closets
and fed it monstrously of coal
and the emptiness of vases.
We left a Cinderella pumpkin
on the brick walk and it disappeared
in less than a season.
Stole the water first, the seeds
papered to eyelids, the shape

drew toward its center, shrunk
down to a skin that too withered away
until there were only the bones
of a lizard who had hunkered
beneath its stagecoach frame.

The Snow Leopard Mother

The snow leopard mother runs straight
down the mountain.
Elk cliff. Blizzard.
Hammers keening
into the night.
Her stillness and wild
falling is a compass
of hunger and memory. Breath
prints on the carried-away body.
This is how it goes so far away
from our ripening grapes and lime,
coyote eyes rimming the canyon.
Yet
we paddle out in our ice boat
headed toward no future at last.
O tired song of what we thought,
silence crouches like a prow.
We break the ice gently forward.
If I want to cling to anything
then this quiet of being the last
to know about our lives.

4

(PART FUR PART HOLLOW)

Foxlogic, Fireweed

When I say it breathed inside the house
I mean I felt the air swell around me.
I was upstairs; it was behind me.
I was downstairs; it was roiling across the room.
From all angles, I was turned.
When I say it breathed
I mean also that it shrieked, the sound
so dislocating and new, it was heat
and certainty like steam shearing up
out of the earth, like lightning
branding snow.
My feet were strange to me.
My hands careless and flimsy.
It was behind me, at my neck
as if I could reach out and tremble
its vapors. I was circling,
my arms lifted when I saw
the tribe of foxes
press at the back door
searing their cries upward into the house.
We locked in awe, wild eyes
until the darkness stole us
back to our separate worlds.

Tinderbox

A grove of orange trees. Fog-and-crow sky.
Ant trail leading in or out.
We follow no path, hold hands. You are just
old enough for me to ask what you dreamt about
when you laughed yourself awake and returned, wake
and turn, pull of the conscious rowing you back
too often, too soon—*a little whale inside a tunnel*—
we have learned night has eight keys and too
many locks. You want to know if the palm
branches are dead enough to pick up. You drag
heavily behind, comb sandshorn lines.
I am trying to feel now what I will remember
afterward, what you will not. How we touched
the crowded leaf scars—*every tree's a living fossil.*
At two, I tell you everything if not for knowledge
then the mystery of maidenhair, sleeping gingko,
tinderbox. You are sweeping now.
You are courteous with the dead.
Lathe and rasp. Last slake of ash
in the hollowed rind. When you say it is amazing,
I know it is amazing. Little bowls with their wet light.

Making Use

My grandmother could do it, yours,
in a threadbare kitchen, pull from the compost
onionskins, zucchini stumps, damp ribbons
of peeled carrot, into the stockpot
she could bathe the babies in,
add the gristle, the discarded bone;
if she waited long enough, hymn by hymn,
the water might draw out one last savory breath.
Sieving up the fibrous, the wrack of husks
with midwifery hands, the family sustained.
And if there was one pillow and three children
she would open the seam and divide,
shear into the hand-me-down quilt,
patterns for teddy bears.
Sour milk softened bathwater, a bowl of coffee grounds
on the counter after a fish fry, old bread folded
into a pudding or bagged for a day at the pond.
The lineage of making use an informal art
quietly gathered, mended by example:
salt dough, wood ash lye water,
my mother sewing dresses out of pillowcases.
Women make use of almost anything
worthy of a little left life.
My friend returning from the NICU
takes out the flour and sugar at midnight
and blends in the rotten bananas without thinking,
suddenly in the blue kitchen waiting for the bread to rise.
The artist who works in lint, sculpts an entire exhibit
of bunnies from dust bunnies,
and Georgia O'Keeffe once said

I got half-a-dozen paintings out of that broken plate.
Old boot, reckless childhood, chronic fatigue,
empty house, blight, this clock set to winter,
I can fire this train wreck in the kiln
and eat from the bowl of it.
So unsung this work of sensing life cycles,
knowing how to resuscitate, and by way
of transformation, coax forward, and yet so expected
that less than a day after a person who will become
our president is caught bragging of sexual assault
as if he has not already bragged it many times over,
the cue to glean out the usefulness is everywhere:
opportunity for women to speak up,
best thing that could have happened,
he opened the door.
Door to a room that we were born into
nothing opening but his terrible mouth.
If we choose to talk,
if we write a letter about how it happened,
if together we make a list:
at a party, on a city street in broad daylight,
a Greyhound bus, a family reunion,
a wedding, a state forest, in a business meeting . . .
if we close the accordion screens and buckle in the grief,
know these are our own actions and not
a form of tending the call, know
we have long ago made what is to be made
and we know when to hum the prayer of discernment
for the broken, when to cull out the good
and when to rot the corpse back to its bones.

Altar: Fairytale

A house on chicken feet.
In the belly of a thick soup.
Leaves blackened to crows.
Loaves of bread buried in the loam.
A cave dripping honey.
Softly breaking sticks suggesting hands
and a fire's struck hiss.
How you folded into the hollow,
candled and warm, the tree lit against
itself, amberblack crawling back
into the original story.

A Deer Story

One night while his son was in college,
a man died in his sleep. First, breathing;
then not. Apnea, the reports later explained,
the body shutting itself off in the night

like a thermostat. After the friends and neighbors
cantered in and out of their living room, after
the monochromatic casseroles they fed
to the dogs, after his mother started drinking

again, his sister binge-eating in the dark,
everyone shameful in the house,
the son, an art student who didn't return
to college, lugged on his father's

hunting clothes, took the rifles and his girlfriend
out to the woods. Empty world, to empty
it more, prove he still had a little god
in his hands. She marched behind him

through the grasses, sat with him by the rock
wall for hours. She who had said so little, again
said nothing, blurry outside her skin
watching the texture of each husked minute.

Autumn. Everything curling into itself.
When the buck emerged in the brush,
eight points, a direct line, the rifle
cocked to kill, she did not speak or touch him

but held the air around him. Cruelty
and its cousins, retribution and grief;
this had nothing to do with her. And yet.
Was she an accomplice in bearing witness?

An accomplice in hoping she might stop it?
The moment before clicked again and again,
time raised above them, spring-loaded,
their three bodies bent toward each other

wildly alive. When the animal heart released
itself to the air in an abandonment of silence,
he lowered the rifle and treaded back.
I would have done it if you weren't there,

finally in the truck. Did it answer something,
to stage a death and save it from himself?
And the girl was me, further then,
from his regret or loneliness or anger,

I could not enter it, riding away
with the velvet body warm inside me,
its fleeing a door that swung open,
its body my body at last unto itself, awake.

Still Life with Skeleton and Sight Word

Halloween trinket that keeps resurfacing.
A child's studied word slipped from the stack.
She seems to be saying it
drawn to the jaw as mantra
(see how the word suggests sentience, *she*).
A soft opening, part fur part hollow
as a tongue between the teeth
narrows into ellipse.
To sing it is a *wind-in-the-throat*
to pray: *though I walk in the valley*
An apology:
though I have no tongue
though if I were, that I would be so disordered
or a grace: the word *breath* loosening
part concession: *though we have little to offer*
part sigh: *though the road be long*.
Longing to be whole as a body
maybe a word is a beginning, a small flesh.
We could make of ourselves a heavy bell together
swing it forward, back
as light drains the room
our *Though Bone Though Bone*
quieting what little of day, done.

Vigil

San Bernardino, California, December 2, 2015

After the shooting,
after the helicopters-for-days
circled our house
then left,
the owls we'd never heard but must have
been there all along
leaned in
toward the house;
like lamplight
homed toward our small
predictable messes, saying what
we could not, the body's bellow,
choral from the damp cedar
from the hard planks of the heart—
there are two hearts:
one for kindness, one for grief—
and their staying in
had nothing to do with us,
the figures in the house, tending
though their calls felt like sap
easing the shock,
but because they'd been opened
to their own kind
of terror in the air
they lowered to our windows, watchful,
tuning the wrecked sky
back to stillness.

How Many Leaves and Boats Gather Together

Buoy the blue
night, small boats lifting
beyond the layers of *tremble* and *tree*.

We are the watchers of the world,
the notetakers, the lonely captains
sailing over the good earth.

Meanwhile, the birds fly west—
   if they had a religion it would be
   the agreement of flight—

      and fish swim east in silver wheels
      through a horizon of slow-blooming sound.

Leave the moonlight to itself,
what little may be answered.

Let night whisper into the hull
of your ear
the other language.

Dark wildwood,
that we ride silently
into the harbor

alone and no one sees—
arrival or departure—
but that it matters

to be briefly carried
to so close a place as home
on such a thin and flickering sea.

Cabinet of Curiosities

The cabinet itself with its hapless knobs
and vectors or perhaps each drawer and glass case
was added one by one as every pocket ruin
was recovered from its afterlife:
penile bones of rodents aligned
in a miniature xylophone,
sheet music penned to a saltine.
The dozen of us gathered to witness
a dodo bird shellacked into bewilderment
next to the rare jellyfish jar
like two washed-up actors in a halfway house
and what could we really say about the ossuary
of books bleached into bone dust,
the thousands of years for each word
to rub itself off the page. Between cotton
boxes and jars of brine, a kind of faith
in trying to pin mortality's wings against black
felt and I wondered what offering an occasion
of strangeness is beyond the tidy fact
of having seen it though I recall childhood
days after rain when I'd dig
just for the accident of the odd
stone I wanted to call *arrowhead*, to say
my effort had added to the recovery
of the world. No chatter
but the gesture of fingers,
admission tickets crisp in hand
as photos snapped to save what had been saved,
photos that will go extinct in their formless
digitalia. These burdens

of memory, glued and glassed,
I wanted relic to return to wreckage
and nothing to last beyond
my small margins of dust.

What Turkeys Can Teach Us about Grief in Suburbia

That it moves in circles, that you don't need to be poised
or eloquent, the pressure scouring you
to orate by noon the true and succinct words
vastly-with-all then vastly-alone
stuffed with food or void of it, the coffee too hot
in the thin Styrofoam the coffee so cold in the night-pot.
The turkeys advise against polarity or wisdom.
Walk with us our upland kind, steady
the loop of our walking under the crisscross
wires, under the live oak and the story of its rustling.
To be swept in a quiet shape together around any small death:
fender-struck cat, being of our being,
what fallen birdlet we never knew.
We gather the pieces
of each other and walk them round
the cul-de-sac, one holding what the other cannot.
The procession need not advance
nor march toward any heavy door waiting to close.
Let the ownership of grief be the shadow of a wheel
and its moving parts and if one sounds
the rattling drum from the well we bow
our necks and sound the terrible
beauty that weeps us, body we knew or
body we could never understand which once
we heard yowling in the night, crouched and feline
like a locked spring, we watched the magnificent
creature leap toward the sound of its mousetrap throat
and our hearts shuddered open in our baskety bodies.

We watched the dark fur of it fly toward itself,
claw-thing, no wings anywhere,
limp-dead street, the lights creaking on at dusk.
Round and round, oh moon what are we to do
with all these feathers?

5

(IN A CIRCULAR WIND)

bike shed will often show more results than "bike shed"

Whale song will often be louder than *"whale song"*
as *flower girl* runs faster into the field than *"flower girl"*
and *star dust* settles more thickly than *"star dust."*
Fish stick will often know more of fish than *"fish stick"*
and *beach glass* will often know less of the sea than *"beach glass."*
Draw fire away from its place, rain from coat, milk from man.
Let light in
that strangeness may be
reassembled by the breath
that a bike be a shelter that a shelter carry us off on slim wheels
that riding is a condition of leaving
that some fearsome thing always comes loose in a circular wind.
Unhemming the couple
one pauses to see the thing in its own delicate spiral,
this cannot be helped.
You with your sturdy distance, I with my mud shoes and water spicket,
how I want to part them now ecstatically the mud and the shoes
the table and the spoon, the air and the port
and zoom down the center aisle with you
shedding ourselves of bikes and stars and plans.

Antlers

Out of velvet, winter.
Out of the center, the idea splits.

Wilder stars, my eyes leap
my head is soft,

it does not end here in the cleft
between my ears:

fragment, dream, map that arrows
in the mist.

In the widening fields I become
silent, a stillness

that makes light in spring
harden into branches.

Say: *what I will bear.*
What flanked impulse swells in me.

Mothbone, amulet,
the milked horn

flares.
I go sky, crown

in all directions.
Run like a tree

into the wind.

For the brown widow who laid her eggs under my son's bicycle seat

You are searching the domed
curves of shelter, a haunt
of darkness to forge

    a pair of eggs larger
    than your body.
    Anchor and parachute,

wisp and captor,
you cast your nets
cast and cast all directions

    then time unspools before you.
    Under lip of flowerpot
    a lawnchair's crook

against the weighted clanger
of the chime,
I've never spotted your starry

    orbs without your fiddleback
    your hollow mouthparts
    perched in the filigree.

How I've dug the stick in
crushed the papery shells into dirt
then pulled you through the wreck.

    My apology is thin. I don't know
    where to let you live.
    He practiced in the driveway.

It only took a few yards
before he found the midpoint,
that precarious balance of belief

in the center of everything.
One foot pushes off
and the other pumps back,

divine symmetry.
I took him out to the track
where once he circled, he lit,

purposeful. Windmaker,
looping the afternoon to dusk,
how could the sky not

have been an anthem?
He wheeled;
you held. The eggs

spackled in their basket
feeling what of this world.
Laying the bike on its side

we saw your sticky lair,
he had reached under
earlier as he propped himself on.

Had we not dismantled
you would have continued
through the mornings,

the late afternoons,
as he learned how to take a hill
a fall, you would have stayed

until the breaking open
your divine
teal-metal entrance.

A wind here can take
down a litter of palm branches,
overturn the bottle-

    heavy garbage cans
    but you, feathery mass
    of intricate making

remain on such silks
beneath the highway-bound car
the victor of a boy's

    lengthening body
    coming into its power.
    We head indoors and I am sure

you are more with us
than we see
nestled in the stashed corners

    of our lives, mending.
    Under the arch
    of a thirty-year roof

built by whose hands,
we survive beyond
our knowing

    all the wild and immersive
    gestures of the earth
    too large for us to perceive.

Altar: Aerial Heart

blue cloth
a window
thimble of salt
as salt teases out water
as water teases out an echo
as an echo teases out flight
to be received upward
and skyward
beyond the mapped world

Pastoral

If you give me a houseplant, I will write a poem. I will rip the poem into pieces and drop them in a pitcher of water and listen to Joan Baez and make a casserole and swear when I forget about the casserole and it burns. Burning it will remind me about the water pitcher sitting in the window, late-day sunlight filtering through the torn paper, and I will think how this is a much better use of the poem, how a poem should always be submerged and shot with light. I will eat the casserole anyway, and it will take me three days to wash out the crusty pan. I will not shower or pay overdue bills because the minutiae hunkers under a tidal wave called Tuesday, and I will look in the mirror and realize I am submerged and shot with light, which will remind me of the water, the poem now a dull pulp, and I will pour it over the houseplant, which I believe you gave me yesterday, and I will write you a note to tell you how much I love it, how I am taking such kind care of every single thing.

Our Laundry Room of Deflated Balloons

After the streamers have been pulled away to tape stubs,
last stale slice of cake claimed in the night kitchen,
when the presents lie fallow behind couches
and ribbons are gathered in cabinets for a future gift,
the boy drifts backward from the glory,
king of one day, his rule quiets
to a fitful hum and he's lost again
in the work of wanderment and dismantling.
Above our heads, the balloons buoy,
last emblems still cheerful with their silvery
exclamations continue to offer reprise.
He assesses their lift each morning,
cresting above the ribbons he lets them
roam though they pucker and sag;
for weeks hanging on,
melancholy in the breeze
of our walking. When they bow down
to us, head to head, like benevolent
houseguests, nearly sentient,
as if we might give pause to one another
as we pass, he exiles them to the laundry room,
bobbling in the narrow thruway
to join the others, mylar polka dot luster
wrinkled to metallic skin, glinting
birthday flotsam beached in the corner
behind the muddy shoes and wool sweaters
we'll never wash. I know the ritual,

do not question. Maybe it's about not giving up
that last gleam or that he knows diminishment
is a private thing or a thing we make
private because we do not want to see
how slow a work of leaving becomes.

Meeting

Tremble the thin
shock of light
locked in its nightbox.

Come, weathers,
extravagant and wild
licking your fox pups

and sanding them clean.
Frantic in the eyes
we scavenge

with our looking.
I in my nothing-gown
behind the glass

do not hold them
there and have never
been hungry.

Three-Handed Clock

We didn't always know how to make
a house, where to nest
the mail, how many bowls were enough

but not too much, how to locate
the slender cracks where the ants
threaded in. You remember, love,

how painstakingly we chose *pongee*
the adobe paint swatch to transform
our basement apartment to a mesa's warmth

then sitting afterward in the claustrophobia
of our newly fleshy studio. Remember
the dealers underneath our San Francisco

railroad flat and the drag queen who filmed
movies on our shared landing pausing for us
to pass with the groceries or laundry.

Remember the loosed pit bulls, the keg parties,
the undergrad Victorian up in flames
across the street in Michigan. Remember

the teenagers sleeping on our porch in the rain.
And the banana tree we planted outside
our California bedroom that shot upward

like a hurried adolescent then produced its single
flower so leaden with pollen and sex it brought
the whole tree sideways to its death.

Our cache of belongings that has swelled and shrank
and swelled again, boxed and lifted to five different homes—
were they part of us or props we gathered and cast

in their roles? The cobalt pottery, the curtains
hung from thumbtacks, the leaking sink,
crooked bathtub, raccoons that used to brawl

in the alley by our bedroom window.
Remember the bats, the mice, the birds, spiders
we escorted out over and over, and the alligator

lizard who laid eggs in our coat closet
releasing thirteen babies one late August morning?
And when I finally bought a clock for the kitchen,

it was a three-handed clock, the faux rustic design
making of the big hand a diameter, yet we acclimated,
mistelling the time for months before we learned how

to leave a space for the extra hand to measure some other
gradient of belief. What I'm saying is
it's been some time figuring out how to do this,

how to spackle, how to prune, side by side,
how to wake in all these approximate lives
to this one where the wisteria blooms

even though it's not supposed to
and the birds come all day toward our windows.
I love the catalog of our effort readying us

for so many different futures we tried on
but didn't choose and how they all unknowingly
pointed toward this one—the quiet heat

of foxes, your budding makeshift orchard,
in the rain with Q-tips pollinating the cherry tree
by hand before it had a mate. That other axis

of time steadying itself toward the length
of years, and the calmness of another day
laid at our feet in its delicate composition.

Nacelle and Turn

The windmills station the desert
as though they have come here
of their own accord.

Sentience or
indifference, they vessel
and crank *what exactly*

one hundred seasons in a field of quiet
the knowledge of machines
restive and spun,

silent noise of all that motion.
The desert's question is always
what do you want to let go?

Blanch and scree, the vista scoured
clean and you can tumble
your guilt horse, darkest compass

across the playa rearview.
It will wear your leavings down to a howl.
I want to believe in many things—

health, justice, the moon—
but all that wind moving invisibly
it would carve itself

on the rocks if it could.
To see it gathering
circle circle circle,

is to see space flow
how inside the wind there is
something else moving,

I want to believe
this is optimism,
alien world.

Ceremony

I laugh in my sleep and wake
to my luck, that there is coffee
and it is warm and that I have a mouth
is luck. The wet snap of air, empty
breadbox, and paper mountains
that never seem to erode,
they are glorious.
And when each evening a hawk
flies over the house, its shadow too
along this oddly curved wall
flies right over my head.
In some bright city I have quietly escaped
my death without knowledge.
Time I did not stop for the sunset
or did. Having lingered too long at the wedding
because I did not know how to leave.
The procession passed by and devastated
no one but left the shadow of one
granted bell then another.
Skin of an orange. Salvaged book.
Another web spinning in another
unreachable corner.

NOTES

"I will break into my life for my life" is based on the experience of a group of tourists who began an elaborate search party near Iceland's Eldgiá canyon, only to find out later, the missing woman was actually among the search party.

The phrases "I will break into my life for my life," and "brighten the road, dear" are both quotes from Argentine poet Jacobo Fijman's "Vespers of Anguish."

Terezín was a concentration camp thirty miles north of Prague in Czechoslovakia during World War II. Terezín's detainees included renowned scholars, philosophers, writers, dramatists, visual artists, and musicians, who continued to produce art under horrific conditions. A propaganda film was made displaying the façade of a rich cultural life and was shown to the Red Cross. These artists built the railroad that carried them from to Terezín to Auschwitz.

"Jennifers of the 1970s" highlights the 859,112 Jennifers born during the peak Jennifer era.

"In the House of Seals" describes Año Nuevo Island, off the California coast, which had a lighthouse, elaborate keeper's house, and many other structures. The area's elephant seals, nearly extinct from being hunted for blubber, began to repopulate after 1950, and seals, sea lions, and shorebirds took over the vacated buildings on the island, now home to ten thousand seals.

The phrase used as the title *"To Remain in Perhaps,"* comes from the anthology *Lyric Postmodernisms*, in which Bruce Beasley references the Italian expression *rimanere in forse*, "to remain in perhaps." This phrase best captures the state of the lyric poem to me.

"Snake in the Zendo" notes a *zenji*, or Zen master. The poem takes place in Tassajara Zen Mountain Center, Carmel Valley, California.

In "Making Use," the artist who makes bunnies out of dust bunnies is Suzanne Proulx.

"Vigil" was written in the nights after the mass shooting in San Bernardino in 2015 that claimed the lives of fourteen people. One of our friends was shot seven times and miraculously survived and another friend was one of three first responders.

"How Many Leaves and Boats Gather Together" borrows its title from a line in the poem, "Magnolia" by Judith Skillman. Thank you for this beautiful line that I could not stop saying.

The *Wunderkammer* described in "Cabinet of Curiosities" is part of the Strahov Monastery in Prague.

When an Internet search yields no results, this message will often be posted: *bike shed* will often show more results than *"bike shed."* I first encountered this phrase while running an obscure search on the Academy of American Poets' website, www.poets.org, the subject of which I no longer remember, but the phrase was so odd and interesting to me, I wrote the poem instead.

The phrase "aerial heart" is part of one of the boxes in Sara Biggs Chaney's poem "Table of the Elements, girlhood."

WITH GRATITUDE

To Grace Bauer, who said yes. It means everything to me.

To all the wonderful people at the University of Nebraska Press for taking such care with me.

To luminaries Traci Brimhall, Marsha de la O, and Diane Seuss for inspiring me over the years and adding your generous words to this collection.

To my dearest friends in poetry. I only keep a few of you close to me, but Lauren Henley, Joy Manesiotis, Mary Ann McFadden, you are steadfast, talented, full of love and invention and clarity, and I'm indebted to be in conversation with you always.

To Tricia Caspers, Annie Stenzel, Katherine Case. Twenty years ago, we started meeting every two weeks, and though we're spread across the West Coast now, our decade-long poetry group will always be a treasure.

Thank you to my parents who have supported this path and cheered me on and on.

And to my inner circle—Forest, Liam, Chad—you are where the magic happens.

2019   Jennifer K. Sweeney, *Foxlogic, Fireweed*

2018   John Sibley Williams, *Skin Memory*

2017   Benjamín Naka-Hasebe Kingsley,
        Not Your Mama's Melting Pot

2016   Mary Jo Thompson, *Stunt Heart*

2015   Kim Garcia, DRONE

2014   Katharine Whitcomb, *The Daughter's Almanac*

2013   Zeina Hashem Beck, *To Live in Autumn*

2012   Susan Elbe, *The Map of What Happened*

2004   Aaron Anstett, *No Accident*

2003   Michelle Gillett, *Blinding the Goldfinches*

2002   Ginny MacKenzie, *Skipstone*

2001   Susan Firer, *The Laugh We Make When We Fall*

2000   David Staudt, *The Gifts and the Thefts*

1999   Sally Allen McNall, *Rescue*

1998   Kevin Griffith, *Paradise Refunded*

The Backwaters Prize in Poetry was suspended from
2005 to 2011.

To order or obtain more information on these or
other University of Nebraska Press titles, visit
nebraskapress.unl.edu.

CPSIA information can be obtained
at www.ICGtesting.com
Printed in the USA
LVHW020534200121
676902LV00012B/1267